Unfolded

Unfolded

Sumedha Jena

BLACK EAGLE BOOKS
Dublin, USA | Bhubaneswar, India

Black Eagle Books
USA address:
7464 Wisdom Lane
Dublin, OH 43016

India address:
E/312, Trident Galaxy, Kalinga Nagar,
Bhubaneswar-751003, Odisha, India

E-mail: info@blackeaglebooks.org
Website: www.blackeaglebooks.org

First International Edition Published by
Black Eagle Books, 2024

UNFOLDED
by **Sumedha Jena**

Copyright © Sumedha Jena

All rights reserved. No part of this publication may be reproduced, stored in a retrieval system, or transmitted, in any form or by any means, electronic, mechanical, photocopying, recording or otherwise without the prior permission of the publisher.

Cover & Interior Design: Ezy's Publication

ISBN- 978-1-64560-636-9 (Paperback)
Library of Congress Control Number: 2024952718

Printed in the United States of America

Dedicated to all those who have shaped me into the person I am today. I know my journey of growth is far from over, but I am endlessly grateful for every good and bad memory we've shared.

Preface

Writing this collection of poems for this book might have been one of the hardest writing journeys I have been on so far. In the past two years, I have encountered a lot of changes in my life; changes that have enabled me to grow as a person and heal from past experiences that have hurt me. It took a lot of strength for me to be able to express the feelings I had been holding in by writing them down, as I was afraid to feel vulnerable. This book took almost over a year in the writing process, because I was constantly scraping stanzas and poems, essentially unsure of whether it fit with the overall theme of the book. I was initially struggling with balancing college and keeping my thoughts creative enough to write poetry.

    I chose the title of this book as, "Unfolded," because from a reader's point of view it's a series of events from life that are slowly unfolding over a period of time. I went through a temporary depressive arc early into entering university and therefore lacked the motivation to write, eventually falling into a rut. This feeling changed this year, as I encountered new people in my life where we shared new experiences. Because of this, I was able to come out of my shell once again, and really begin to live life the way it was meant to be lived, as opposed to constantly living in a bubble of worry. But nevertheless, once I re-entered the proper headspace to write, I was unable to stop myself. I came to the conclusion that I would be reflecting back on several different eras and circumstances in my life, from the perspective of someone who has grown up in the past couple of years. In this book I write about experiences filled with love, hatred, revenge, peace, fear, and hope, so I can look back at them from a place of serenity and appreciate how far I have come from them.

I start the first poem from the very beginning of my life, hence why I titled it "first breath," because it's my perspective on me being born into this world. I take the reader on a journey to several different times of my life that helped influence my life for the better. I reflect on each of these events with a positive mindset, to attain the closure I need so I can live a more peaceful life going forth. I discuss discovering my identity as an individual who is also figuring out her footing in this world, while navigating the travesties life has to offer. Family bonds and friendship are common motifs across my poems as well, as I mention the strength my family and friends give me and the value of their presence in my life, several times. This is due to my realization that life is too short to be holding a teenage angst or grudge against others, so it is important to treasure the fleeting moments in life before it is too late. I end this book by writing a poem about the gratitude I feel for every individual that had an important impact on my life, whether it be good or bad, because if I hadn't experienced it, I wouldn't be the person I am today. Every experience I have gone through has shaped me into the person I am today, and although I have my imperfections that I strive to improve, I am proud of who I am becoming.

This time around I didn't take any direct inspirations from other renowned poets, as I really wanted my words on these pages to feel raw and genuine. I believe my writing style is different this time around, compared to my previous works. I observed that my sentences have gotten more descriptive in terms of imagery and longer in length, which is an aspect of my writing I am proud of. It is good to see that my current writing mirrors the personal growth I have made as a person as well. Another observation I can make is that the content of my poems this time are more realistic as opposed to conceptual and abstract. Every single piece of writing is based on an actual thought, feeling, or experience I lived through that I decided to reflect upon. I wanted it to be more realistic but also less depressive, so it stood out from my previously published writings. Even if I did start out a poem on a sadder note by following the theme of finding closure and healing, I would incorporate that midway to demonstrate that life is greater than simply focusing on the negatives.

    Overall there is a visible positive trend when it comes to the poetry I have written over the years, and I wanted to truly focus on that in this collection to demonstrate the change a person goes through in the early transformative years of their life. I wanted to thank the editor, Professor and Dr. Satya Sankar Mishra, a retired Professor in English, Govt. of Odisha who aided in revising the words that I have written. With his vision, I was able to arrive at the realization of what the overall theme of my poetry stands for. As always, I would like to thank my family and friends who have constantly enabled and embraced my passion for writing and helped me stay true to that all these years.

A bird's eye-view

On going through the latest craftsmanship of Sumedha's galaxy of poems entitled 'Unfolded,' I feel she is a promising youngster of letters offering an incisive way of writing added to a content that is by and large self—explanatory. The fragments may be taken as a necessary sequel to the first two collections of verses: a kind of signature of what 'had been, has been' and of course, if her determination persists… 'will ever be' in the days to follow.

Looking at the first person singular orientation of her diction and syntax one obviously locates casual, informal yet perceptive uses of words or lines such as, "not a moment spent outside of our bubble" (poem 11) or "memories etched in every nook and cranny" (poem 27) that carry the meaning to the core. Few metaphors like: "this cocoon of a chrysalis" (poem 19) or "a solo odyssey" (poem 29) helps tying up the nostalgic frenzy of the poet. Despite omission of capital alphabets/ letters at the beginning of a line the pieces bring out an automatic display of feelings and ideas as available in the free-verse composed in prose order of its kind: pauses and variations adding to the unstoppable continuity in maintaining a prose order that is totally conversational. However, the crux of her writings has been to explore varied phases of experiences she comes across 'within' and 'even without' herself on shifting from a confined family life to the ethos of a friendly yet meaningful social scenario wherein she achieves an identity of her own. There is a happy acceptance of reality as she sums up: "carrying a part of every soul who has touched my life woven into the fabric of my being" (poem 40).

    I congratulate her for such an endeavor and wish her a prosperous career as a poet.

Dr Satya Shankar Mishra
Former Professor of English and
Former Director, I.A.S. Coaching Centre
Govt.of Odisha, India

CONTENTS

First breath	15
Everlasting	16
Forever family	18
Rooted journeys	20
Forging belonging	22
Fraternal covenant	24
Eternally unbroken	26
Glimpse of bereavement	28
Lessons in solitude	30
Metamorphosis	32
Ephemerality	34
Paper dreams	36
Mind of a perfectionist	37
Cultural crossroads	38
Gilded cage	40
Freshman frontier	41
Bitter harvest	42
Self-theft	43
Freefalling	44
Invisible battles	46
Fleeting euphoria	48
Unveiling aspirations	50
Nature's revival	52
Awaiting adventures	53
Coming of age odyssey	55
Aural oasis	57
Bittersweet farewell	58
Intellectual expeditions	60
The soul's reveries	62
True liberation	63
Renewal	64
Unraveling stone	65
Kindred souls	66
Missing pieces	67
Kinship revelations	69
Savoring victories	71
Imbued in the now	73
Silver fox	74
Never gone too far	76
Blessings in disguise	77

First breath

walls enclosing her like a warm blanket
wrapped in a cocoon filled with love
where a young soul, protected from above, rests
the universe opens up in the mother's embrace
life's gentle whispers, an undiscovered symphony,
within her home, a mysterious music echoes
shrouded in obscurity but wrapped by radiance,
a treasured soul geared to take off
every flicker, a countenance of expectation,
a divine illumination, a whispered exchange
a state of serenity where time is suspended,
the tempo of a heartbeat, steady but aware
a subtle cry that comes with every subtle push
sheltered in her mother's arms, dreaming peacefully
the wonder of this mysterious home draws me in
where destinies emerge and dreams come true
in the womb of all beginnings, the delicate blossom of love,
future memories she will make, lie ahead of her
in the spirit of all life, as she wakes to take her first breath

Everlasting

never knew the feeling of snow
the crisp and cold air, biting gently
soon to infiltrate my lungs
just a child, in winter's touch.

too young to even remember
how the ground blanketed in the purity of white,
yet the feeling of togetherness
remained with me forever

a couple years older and wiser
winter's breath graces my windowpane
creating frozen, serene landscapes
underneath a pale winter sun

schools closed, we are all iced in
relishing winter's allure beauty
the scent of wood smoke in the air
holds a cherished place in my memory

indeed, what a time it was
back when roads would be frozen still
stuck in a moment forever
as the snowflakes dance in the breeze

a mess of snow angels and snowmen

cold noses and rosy cheeks
fragments of my childhood unfold
in frosty mornings and glistening icicles

the biting cold, yet invigorating
invited me for a day of bliss
later admiring the clear, starlit nights
making my youth everlasting

years sail by, the frost returns
excitement surges within me.
running towards the closest door
to see the magic of winter's wonderland

disappointment settles in as I see
the symphony of crackling ice melting
that stillness of a snow-covered forest
vanishing from my eyes

my heart aches for that familiar feeling
where I had no care in the world
each year the inches grew smaller
as I, too, age with the seasons.

the magic steadily dissipates
how I longed to dance in frosty air
embracing the cozy nights by the fireplace
as I recall the everlasting days of my youth

Forever family

I exist alone in the comfort of solitude.
a child alone in my personal universe.
no hysterical laughs from a sibling to fill the silence,
no adventures in tandem, no one to fret over.

wandering and frolicing during my childhood,
yet occasionally my heart would sway sadly.
for a whisper would arise in the quiet,
seeking for more family, beneath the veil of clouds.

others rejoiced in the warmth of their siblings' bond
—a beacon that blazed brilliantly.
they bantered and joked, yet they kept together.
a connection forged since the beginning of existence.

I floated under the shadow of tranquility,
of a friend by my side, as my family
to exchange whispered secrets in the dark,
where fear sets flight to drive shadows away.

day by day, the longing increased,
a profound wanting, a hidden ache.
for the affection of a sibling, a helping hand,
a strand of gold in the great fabric of life.

I whispered to the stars in the nighttime sky.

wishing for a brother to arrive faster.
to accompany me on this journey through life,
together in happiness, together in suffering.

while I treasured the peaceful, quiet times,
having a sibling around felt like an eternity away.
but I harbored a deep-seated desire for a companion.
just a yearning for a forever family

although serene, an only child's life
can resemble an unspoken scream.
but a seed was planted in the recesses of my heart,
a need to have a sibling to call my own

Rooted journeys

my roots sought deep in the heart of my homeland,
traditional streets where I used to stray.
yet fate called us with a whispering breeze,
to begin our voyage across endless skies.

abandoning behind the scent of aromatic air,
boarding a plane, our stories unrevealed.
across massive seas, towards unseen land,
to forge a new route, with my family trailing behind

as visions of America started to take shape.
the skyline of India slowly vanished from sight,
a mixture of adrenaline and anxiety,
as we embarked on, to our destination

a wave of amazement upon arriving
at the land of opportunities and freedom
the pulse of the metropolis, the hustle of this city,
under my feet, there's a fresh beat to dance to.

among the buildings that greeted the sky
I felt a depressive ache in my heart
but I pinpointed my spot in the midst of the confusion,
a celebration of diversity in the melting pot.

it's a navigation of new accents, traditions, and cuisines,
every moment is a cornucopia of sights.
I relished the trek, both day and night,
from the crowded streets to the idyllic park.

as each day went by, I persevered,
a memory weaved, thread by thread, into embroidery.
from the coasts of India to this new world,
a fresh chapter commenced and is immutable.

I found my footing in the country of opportunity,
and I started this journey with courage as my compass.
although I had come a long way from the beginning,
I seized the challenge like a rising sun.

from the hues of Holi to the sparkle of the Fourth,
blending of traditions, such as strokes of paint.
I felt at ease in this tapestry of diversity.
an eternal adventure, an endless embrace.

this country became my new home through and through
as I learnt and grew throughout all of its valleys.
in this strange, wild, and promising world,
I discovered a part of myself with every step.

Forging belonging

I circulate the hallways of a new school,
in a pool of faces; a stranger with a universal sense.
eyes seeking an inviting glance,
searching for a smile to dissolve the fog.

I weave through the web of newfound interactions
between the wooden desks and crammed halls.
every meeting is a chance to form a new connection,
to create a friendship, and gain mutual respect.

unfamiliar with this place, like a fish out of water
cruising the cafeteria, hoping to be drawn someplace
I take my seat amidst the contagious laughter
I must be immune, I drearily sighed.

to all these appearances, I stood alone,
each passing minute led to an increasing heartache.
I simply looked forward to seeing my parents again,
and express to them my desire to never return here.

as the last class eerily arrives at last
my eyes glaze over as the teacher introduces me
but I lock them with someone in the back
an instant warmth spreads across my body

taking my seat and a conversation ensues
through shared interests and shared classes
time allows me to forge new friendships
on the basis of our hushed confessions

the walls begin to crumble each passing day,
new bonds broke through the cracks of earth
discovering a new community in the diversity of faces
each encounter adds more to my life

I navigate and adopt the sudden change
exploring piece by piece, a little more of myself
discerning a brand new place on my own
I steadily stopped being afraid of the unknown

Fraternal covenant

a miniature version of me
waddling around my childhood home
astonishment on my face as I observe him
an extension of my family I grow to love

my heart swells three times bigger at the mere sight
a wish I only ever dreamt of becomes my reality
soon enough, we were inseparable
he became the only thing I anticipated after school.

his doe brown eyes sparkled with curiosity
I wanted to erase his fears and questions
simply supplant them with worldly joy
I was not his mother, but he was still my blood

someone I could rely on through troubled times
I swore not to let rivalry drive a wedge
as taking care of him increased my duties
but I never cared, as he had to be protected

shielded against the dangers of this world
we only have each other to rely upon
there will be moments when we don't align
a temporary shift in the journey of our life

the triviality of our issues seem miniscule
seconds wasted on frivolous battles
when we ought to have been fighting together
a better future awaits us thanks to these revelations

we mustn't waste any more time, I tell him
a unified front will only strengthen our relationship
I abide by my promise to take care of him
fears faded as our bond grew more resilient

for today and forever, we lean on each other
our childhood memories interwoven together
one day we will reflect and reminisce these moments
as we look out into the horizon in our old age

Eternally unbroken

I was just a young girl then,
who did not deserve to experience that hurt,
the kind that left lasting scars till this day
affecting the way I perceived myself forever

the first time I felt the sting of contempt
invisible barriers that wounded me slowly
blunt as a dagger, the words of a stranger,
sniping me, as they vanish in the darkness

faces obscured by the mask of biases,
crudely reminding me I am unlike them
my eyes began to brim with tears,
as no one offered to wipe them away

there was only one of me,
and hundreds that looked like you
our skins might not appear any less alike
yet, we had the same human soul inside of us.

however, that was never enough for you all
the idealism I once had instantly disintegrated
naive to believe I'd be accepted in a foreign land
and the heavy burden of your bigotry was borne

weeks of this seemingly endless torment
was there truly no one else to pick on?
who was I to turn to, that would help me
and disclose to them about my worst fear coming true?

my days turned into a dreadful nightmare,
so I resorted to my dreams as an escape hatch
these dreams led me to an epiphany
that I needed to become my own savior

tenacity did emerge from the ashes left,
by the flames they tried to burn me down with.
and it bloomed like a flourishing flower
whose roots dug deep into this earth.

I refuse to submit to the same treatment again
though the evidence of my agonizing scars may remain,
my shield rises to defend me once more
and the strength within reignites to fight

Glimpse of bereavement

it began with a casual Sunday morning
a day like any other previously experienced
except there was an eeriness in the air
as horrible news awaited me that forenoon

I saw my parents huddled together
my presence, met with an unnerving silence
several others crowding around in my house
my mind was plagued with unanswered questions

I was taken back inside my room by my mom
and she gently relayed the following words:
your grandmother passed away yesterday
it seemed like my whole world fell off its axis

grief is an oddly strange sensation
one doesn't know how to respond to it,
even though it is staring right at you
suddenly, my soul left my body temporarily

there's a disoriented expression frozen on my face
the only word that left my mouth was, *Oh.*
I often recall that exact moment
since I know I could have said more

I was told we would depart for India soon
and I couldn't comprehend any of this.
I was worried that there was a problem with me,
as my face was continuously left expressionless

however, only if people knew,
the anguish and turmoil that was creating a brew
within my mind, that it rendered me paralyzed
I tried, then, to be resilient for my family.

everything went south when we arrived there
after two years, I finally saw my grandmother.
but it was vastly different from before,
as her vitality drained from her, where she laid.

that's when every wall I put up, promptly came apart
every memory with her suddenly unfolded
tears upon tears constantly flowed out of me
I became an unconsolable and uncontrollable mess

the concept of death seems surreal
how does someone simply leave this earth
and leave behind all their loved ones
to suffer and grieve for years to come

grief arrives to us in different forms
time elapses and the longing remains poignant.
it is a healing route, although the scars still survive
so we endure the pain, as love always prevails

while I accept I lost my grandmother
I realize my father lost his own mother
and as I let that realization slowly sink into me
I go hug my parents a little tighter this time.

Lessons in solitude

unsettling emotions riding a wave within
my gut churned with a raging clamor.
staring with discerning eyes into a sea of faces,
looking for a welcoming harbor, a comfort to cherish.

I grasped the mic with trembling hands,
the words suffocating in the back of my throat.
felt like the world was crumbling, an apocalyptic scene,
my humiliation on display, a raw and vulnerable mien.

sweat cascaded like a river, drenching every pore,
my body, a traitorous core, betrayed me.
disorganized thoughts, control slipping through
and the cold talons of terror gripped in that instant.

unbidden tears welled up, bursting the emotional dam.
I ran off the stage, running from the unwavering pain.
seeking refuge in quiet, to retreat and heal,
believing this to be the lowest moment of my life

however, ten years later, the clarity of hindsight reveals,
the drama I ascribed is but an illusion.
years have passed, the memory faded, a specter laid to rest,
for it wasn't the cataclysm my mind had once possessed.

the world did not end, and I did not stop being,
it was but a fleeting moment, a tempest in a teacup's sea.
a perspective lesson, an incentive to accept,
that our fears, though real, need not dictate our pace.

Metamorphosis

desperately craving a sense of stability
can't handle my ever changing environment
going from one place to another
is simply not my cup of tea

        the ceaseless flow of time whirls
        I am ensnared in the fury of a storm.
        Change becomes an unwelcome guest
        knocking on my door at every opportunity

        the turn of the tides constantly shift
        with each movement they pull me back in
        nothing exists to anchor me to shore
        having to confront the unpredictable waves

I feel a tug of war at every turn,
pushing in vain, refusing the pull.
like a prisoner shackled, I wrestle and resist
seeking to strive for security in spite of chaos.
all of a sudden, a switch flipped in my head

        unwillingly and slowly start to understand
        that change constitutes freedom.
        in its continual movement, I breathe.
        accepting disarray, and finding repose.

each turbulence allows me to rise above
a sprout of strength born from suffering.
in the embers of change, I unearth my power,
a phoenix emerges from the ruins of the night.

although the force of my body repels it
its lessons liberate me, as I cherish them
I dance to the tunes of change to find my place
welcoming the journey grit and grace.

Ephemerality

once upon a quiet, summer's day
hand in hand we would walk alongside
skipping down the cobblestone path
promises of everlasting friendships were born

going from barely knowing you
to never imagining life without your existence
spreading joy to those who come across
bringing the life out within each other

how each star aligns in a constellation
forming a perfect union with one another
the mask falls off in your presence
I sit there barefaced, so you accept me

not a moment spent outside of our bubble
chapters unfolding from the story of our life
each line unraveling a brand new adventure
excited to have that connection forever

sadly that's simply a far-fetched fairytale
as quickly winds change direction
the distance between us quickly increases
no magnet in the world could pull us together

we even exchanged our numbers, however
those eventually lessened by the day
a couple weeks easily turn into months
the phone stopped ringing altogether.

I am at a new school this year
is what I wished to desperately tell you
but what good would that do me
since my absence never affected you

afraid to forge a new friendship
thought our connection was distinctive
I didn't want others to share what we had
and I called you my *best friend.*

contained no regrets about our shared times
and why would I?
when you were my first friend here
first to ever make me feel confident

but ten years older, nonetheless wiser
your face appears as a hazy memory
impossible to recognize you in a crowded room,
and I can't remember your name anymore

Paper dreams

ink blots into each scripted letter
my words overflow down the pages
a passion-fueled anger leads me here
my voice only heard by my paper and pen
the heartbreak felt in each written line
feels a bit dramatic looking back
but bitterness welcomed me like a warm hug
a dark cloud loomed over my head
couldn't shake that invisible rain off
merely anticipated when I'd be home
swiftly pulling my journal out
noting down the voices afflicting my mind
my chest feels lighter with each sentence
puzzled on why I feel this way
my soul gets pulled into the pages
an imaginary world that I created
elysian; would be one way to describe it
how could a land so perfect be born,
from words written so tragically
I was just a child feeling this deeply
but my words were powerful enough
able to absorb the hurt I sensed
a sensation strong enough, it disappeared
whilst the ink remained forever on the page,
my pain dissipated as they sank in
realizing this was the getaway I needed
I keep jotting down my thoughts.

Mind of a perfectionist

is everything I have accomplished even real?
a persistent question that makes my mind spin.
irrespective of how well I perfect every task,
a part of it appears incomplete, like a hollow mask.

if even the tiniest divergence from my vision happens,
my mind sinks into a maelstrom of chaos.
a conflated mess, a maze with no exit,
as the weight of imperfection becomes overwhelming.

the slightest faults, little specks in the vast design,
become enormous chasms that make my confidence waver.
agonizing over every imperfection and error,
drowning in self-doubt, a cycle I can't break.

when someone dares to point out the flaws I see,
I shatter within, adrift in a stormy sea.
not knowing how to respond, how to face the truth
paralyzed by the fear of revealing my lack of proof.

for me, nothing is ever completely enough.
perfection is an elusive goal, a continuous uphill climb
hushed whispers of me not deserving this praise.
and that they'll see through my well created labyrinth.

despite the tumult, a spark of optimism still remains.
telling me my worth isn't defined by these confines.
to hush the critic, to accept the journey's tortuous course,
and take comfort in the beauty of imperfection's dwelling.

Cultural crossroads

jekyll and hyde got nothing on me
perpetually split on which identity to wear
put the wrong shoe on the wrong foot
and I might just make a fool of myself

walking on eggshells in front of family
so I don't come off as supercilious
a label they decided to place on me
a rusted crown that I don't wear proudly

traditional attire doesn't erase the tension
my culture, which is more radiant than the stars
seemed to be dulled by my desperate need,
to be accepted by this country's people

uncomfortable in my own skin now
but did I really wish to shed my identity,
leave it all behind and move forward?
as an American girl with no ties to her past

code switching based on who I speak to
was it truly a place free from judgment
or were my assumptions, my delusions?
wasted enough time worrying over futility.

the place may change but the girl shouldn't.
why avert my eyes if they see me differently
a nation thriving in the richness of diversity
a blend of all cultures arrive at a mixture

a balance achieved in the conflict of traditions
and while I battle to blend in on both sides
side by side, while I traverse identities.
for I find my footing in my individuality

Gilded cage

a fiercely intense dynamic
taking a step forward, but going backwards
when do I get to leave my home
the place that once guarded me
sheltering my dreams and ambitions

standing in the shadows of a shattered home,
cowering in my corner, unsure of my future
constant back and forth--an endless cycle
a piece of me cracks with every clash
longing for solace, for a way forward.

an unreachable dream; of ever leaving
away from the echoes of drifting voices.
the shackles that bind me, wistfully rust
a gilded orb of hope within my grasp
so I may wave adieu to the life built here

a glimmer of hope appears out of hiding
leaving the shell of a broken home in its wake
the possibilities it offers have me enthralled.
I gleefully lie awake as night falls
It'll be over soon enough, I quietly whisper.

Freshman frontier

it's unlike the movies, I quietly mused
perplexed, I entered this strange new world
just a year older, yet I am worlds apart,
hurled into the fray with a palpitating heart
everything was bigger, more imposing,
overnight sensations and saturated with love.
but there I was, an outsider, uncertain,
eager to fit in and discover my allure.
feeling ill-equipped for what lay ahead of me.
a rush of terror, while separated from friends.
all alone to maneuver this unusual place,
this is the trial which defines my future
a hefty burden resting on my shoulders.
an uneasy flutter tinged with thrill,
it's an electric surge, a feeling to satiate.
a foreboding grasp of four years to transpire.

Bitter harvest

was all that effort worth nothing in the end?

eyes that are heavy with malaise
gazing at the soaring horizon above

while i am tethered to this earth
since all I did was keep trying

and pushed myself beyond limits,
where I exhaust myself to the utmost

yet confronted with results that yield no gains.
and I question why I even tried at all

If only I could glimpse of what lies ahead,
to save myself the time, the tears.

recurrent defeats, an inexorable flow,
must I simply feign elation, and let it slide?

my entangled ideas lie dormant,
physically incapable of tolerating any more.

tell me if it was all worth nothing in the end.

Self-theft

spirits
torn by harsh words.
compared, demeaned, shattered
why can't they just accept me?
crushed soul.

Freefalling

feet faltering, but my heart takes the fall,
heart and mind dispersed, bewildered by all
an intricate web of feelings arose,
my head twisted, leaving me in discord.

walls that once thrived now dissipate
crumbling defenses, I let them collapse.
then your essence emerges, radiant and real,
my eyes glisten, immersed in your virtue.

warmth encircles me, flushes my cheeks,
your blazing fire conveys what words cannot.
defenses weaken and barriers erode
my soul has nowhere to hide in your splendor.

an emotion so intense, surreal in its delight,
were only dreams, now a chasm on earth.
our paths interweave from shared roots,
fated branches crafting heavenly love.

in tandem we ascend, an evergreen pair.
nourished by the land we each dwell.
dreams materialize in the respect of reality.
a future we continually envision.

feelings so overwhelming they smother the air,
has this snare ever drowned anybody else?
yet, secure in this haven that we've created,
where new worlds commence and luck entwines.

hidden from the gales that lash outside,
lacking ambiguity, we inscribe our own fate.
this cocoon of a chrysalis that encloses us both,
nurtures the exquisite rebirth.

with you, the purest essence of love pours.
and my head finds solace on your shoulder
an endless serene landscape; the route of our future,
how I wish to seize this treasured moment forever

Invisible battles

at birth, a blank canvas, naive to the world,
but life's burdens mount, compounding their worth.
the weight grows steadily with each passing year
ceaselessly bearing down, obscuring innocence.

a gradual heaviness descends over the psyche.
beyond our reach, invisible forces are conspiring.
perfectly imbalance, the scales tip dramatically,
our equilibrium degrades, as we struggled

the trials of life rise like a surging current,
corroding the coasts where our peace formerly dwelt.
this uphill battle that seems insatiable
yet a valiant heart still seeks to flourish.

the fires of motivation, once blazing but now dull,
each inhale is an agony as perilous thoughts swallow me.
the mind betrays, exhibiting an encompassing power
sparse oxygen on this relentless path.

a interminable battle rages in the depths of the mind,
to give in to the darkness or to life's comforts?
perched precariously on the knife-edge of existence,
torn between moving forward or taking that final ledge.

the decision is daunting, a crucial fork in the path,
will the correct path be taken or lead to darker roads?
the covert whispers of doubt, a shrewd memento,
wondering if one gets closer or mere with each stride.

I wait for the storm to pass with unwavering resolve.
no longer willing to put up with this growing heft.
my battle continues, yet I don't have to go it alone.
for warmth and vitality have been woven into kindred.

the hourglass of this life ultimately fades away
it's futile to live in isolation amid despair.
I desire for a hand to hold through the journey.
a fellow traveler who makes each day better.

the wind makes its way towards a distant dawn,
but together our strides will forge new horizons.
united, our heavy burdens seems less daunting
as the consolation of communion precludes all sorrow.

Fleeting euphoria

a day I dreaded, yet could scarcely conceive,
I can't fool its ominous shadow as it approaches.
what had been endless conversations, a soul salve,
blurs into transient souvenirs, beyond my control.

your visage, with every scar and shape seared into my mind.
fades slowly, as if swept away by the harsh gusts of time.
from being the center of my universe and all I had,
To a veiled obscurity, into which my heart has been cast.

how enigmatic that the one who knew all of me,
could flee to desolate streets where strangers' footsteps echo.
I offered my purest love without any fears or limits.
just to be tossed aside, my soul extracted

though we were adjacent, a split started to silently emerge.
a decaying intimacy that I could feel clearly cease.
I felt your soul's departure coursing in my leaden heart.
loves once spoken tenderly, retreating from each other.

can bitter grudges be used against unlearned actions?
two novice souls lost in the confusing labyrinth of love.
captivated by emotions we couldn't even begin to handle,
oblivious of the deluge that may destroy our hearts

no more latent resentment smolder from the flames
I deny the long-extinguished embers of anger.
as you were the one who first revealed the grandeur of love,
allowing my heart to flourish in that intimate tender.

despite its temporary nature, I remain thankful,
to have been immersed in the rays of love, however fleeting.
an exquisite grasp on beauty's fundamental nature,
a soul that awakens from its quiescence of slumber.

treasured memories we can never lose together,
of euphoria and bliss from love that words can't express.
that pristine success cannot be marred by ghosts of hatred.
love's ultimate manifestation, undiminished, it shines.

when the seasons drifted into years without you around,
your voice started to gradually recede, all distorted.
the beloved inflections that initially gave my name life,
now fall through the hourglass of waning fame like grains of sand.

recollections that once tore at my soul like rainfall of misery,
their sting grows less severe due to time's heartless reign.
once a flood that swept me away in grief's tumultuous wake
now dwindles into a serene sea where curative waters flow.

finally, the leaden weight that made it difficult for me to breathe,
broke free of its hold, enabling me to return to daylight.
every breath flows organically, freely, and unrestrained.
the capacity to be, is restored, as a fresh dawn rises over

Unveiling aspirations

the quicksand of uncertainty grasps at my feet,
keeping me entrenched in the blues.
reaching out, I find no solid ground to meet,
the road ahead has been marred by distractions.

nervously, I speculate where this route could go.
my thoughts stalled, unable to devise a way out.
stagnant, I struggle to break free from this need
to identify the unknown, to locate a clear source.

a mundane cycle continues day after day,
leaving me in a state of mental exile.
I strive to dispel the mist that distorts my future.
looking for the path that might lead me to the peak.

while everyone else seems to be in their element,
I'm disoriented and am unsure what to do.
when will that elusive drive light my dismay,
steering me towards a revitalized life?

I ponder what my future has in mind,
lost in the uncertainty that depresses me.
the absence of direction leaves me feeling icy,
wishing for a passion to be newly found.

I've had this burning desire my entire life.
to give voice to the voiceless, aiding the poor.
relieving the sting of sorrow, this need in me
is this the place where I am meant to be?

the urge to lend a hand, console the suffering,
has been ringing true for a long time in my soul.
this is my creed; serving others and easing pain.
Is this the path that will make me truly whole?

at last, this path ahead is apparent to me.
my purpose in life is this vocation to wellness.
and now no longer disoriented and anxious
I'll pursue this passion, and find my worthy fame.

Nature's revival

vernal arising
frost's icy grip surrenders
petals burst forth, bright

Awaiting adventures

I entered these halls, a mere child, wide-eyed,
but now I leave, wise past my years, into the world.
four years of challenges, perpetual struggles to abide
as soon as we reach this finish line, the stress lifts.

the strain of competition, formerly quite great,
now rises as we celebrate this tremendous feat.
the daunting path, fills me with no fear,
for the knowledge received has fulfilled my spirit.

sensing no longer the innocence of youth,
I stand tall, equipped to face what life may bring.
this chapter closed, a new dawn heralds the truth
that I'm prepared to take flight and widen my wings.

we are drawing to an end, yet a new day is herewith.
a bittersweet farewell as we go our own ways.
our newfound ties bid each other goodbye.
to explore and preserve our uncharted days.

the ambiguous and perilous route ahead,
as immense goals that we ought strive toward now.
though parting brings a touch of anxious fear,
our dreams aim to permeate the future.

at this juncture in our lives, we are together.
preparing for tackling unseen hurdles
now we take to the skies and let our legends shine.
as we walk across that stage--hand in hand.

Coming of age odyssey

at the stroke of twelve, I've attained adult status
yet inwardly, I still feel like a child.
just a day's distinction, as this title grants,
however, the sense of obligation is abruptly great.

society now believes me to be all-knowing,
imposing the same obligations that my parents bear.
however, I was inept for this sudden profound shift
this change from carefree youth to unknown burdens.

I yearn for that lost sensation of lightness.
when worries of life felt faraway versus nearby.
this "adulthood" erases my youthful brightness,
as I confront a future that concerns me today.

I remain residing in the house of my youth.
enclosed by the familiar environs of family.
yet now I'm obliged to sever these ties and wane
stepping out into an unknown from all that is known.

like a fledgling, pushed from its nest's embrace,
wings unsteady enough to attempt their first flight.
as I leave this safe sanctuary, I enter a frontier terrain.
lost and reflecting, "where do I go from here?"

the security I've always known, now parts.
and the chill of untested freedom has taken its place.
perched on this cliff, my trepidation starts.
must I now extend my wings and float into the world?

enveloped by the love of family as I gaze out,
inspiring me to travel, the world's wonders to witness.
but I know their unwavering support will remain
and I feel poised and brave, after this reassurance

their gentle love gives me a license to venture out.
to broaden my scope and discover what life has to offer.
though striking out on my own, I'm never truly alone,
for their undying devotion will never fade.

this safety net of family, which I treasure,
bolsters my confidence to meet the rigors of maturity.
no longer do I view the future with apprehension and,
but lifted by their guiding hands, full of joyful expectancy.

must acknowledge that my life has only just begun.
that transition is an essential rite of passage.
ignoring my unease, I'll rise to overcome obstacles.
I am enticed to value the liberty of adulthood.

Aural oasis

music, the gateway drug to my soul
an energy that courses through every nerve.
a pulsating vibration, making my senses whole,
giving my feelings a happiness I might not deserve.
but then to hear it live, up close and raw,
from the artist whose craft I so deeply admire-
a surreal experience that surpasses every expectation
a sensation I've never felt, so visceral and real.
the raucous rhythms, the melodies that ascend,
they envelop my being, striking a chord deep within.
this harmony with music, an electrifying hold,
unlocks emotions I scarcely knew existed
the stage's dazzling light is engulfed by the admiring crowd.
their fervent energy is transparent in the air.
our voices blend together in perfect ecstasy.
singing each lyric with an unparalleled spirit.
this shared experience, a communion of sound,
transcends the boundaries that divides us
from every corner of the world, we gather around,
we are drawn together by heartfelt music
a bond made by the power of the artist's impassioned art
In this moment, we are no longer strangers
but affiliated entities, united by melodies that fulfill us.
the stage may separate us physically,
but in this exchanged euphoria, we are one.
our voice as an ensemble gleefully rises.
recognizing the music that has emerged victorious.
a real revelation, a moment of transformation--
of music's ability of transportation to another dimension

Bittersweet farewell

a safe haven with four walls, a sanctified place,
a comforting embrace of an oasis, where I might find peace.

when the world seemed cruel and defeat was imminent,
these walls offered refuge, a place to shed a tear.

mumbled secrets, softly spoken admissions,
bearing witness, as if they had grown their own.

memories etched in every nook and cranny,
echoes of laughter, tears, and times uncanny.

the mattress, a canvas for dreams unattainable,
but in those brief minutes, they were so realistic.

within these confines, whimsy and fun danced.
making the cleanest of lines impressions on my psyche.

each poster, each painting, an essence of me,
fragments of my being, for all eyes to see.

once-loved, now fading pictures of faces
ghosts of the past, their bonds slowly degraded.

haunting reminders of who I used to be,
spectral renditions, indelible in my memory.

witnessing my growth, year after year,
this room, a time capsule, holding memories dear.

up until the time came for me to go,
leaving behind these walls that held my heart.

a melancholy farewell, the close of a chapter,
however, the markings they left will always remain.

Intellectual expeditions

spacious pathways, unusual faces all around,
a vast world unrecognizable from the one I knew.
in this unaccustomed land, I am a stranger.
yet excitement stirs, as new knowledge comes into view.

these vacuous faces, devoid of any prior bond,
represent an unexplored field of possibilities.
though initially alarmed, I now feel drawn
to celebrate the prospect of a new identity.

no longer confined to my former, comfort zone,
I stand eager to embark on this profound quest.
the sprawling campus, a canvas yet to be shown -
I eagerly await what lessons it can offer,

though ambiguity lingers, I refuse to be deterred,
as initial unease is outweighed by the lure of progress.
I'll march forth courageously, my soul now awakened.
to capture my journey's subsequent chapter here.

the shift from graduation, a drastic change I face,
as we are all walking into equal, unfamiliar terrain.
fresh encounters await, new connections to cherish -
a rollercoaster of a journey that I eagerly anticipate.

no longer confined by the familiar routine,
I must now learn to pave my own path
stepping out that door with a determined demeanor,
keeping my head up to avoid becoming lost.

in its place is a freedom that both thrills and terrifies.
the regimented routine of earlier years has disappeared.
it is up to me to traverse this unmapped array,
alert to prevent being enticed in by deceptive attractions.

however, I tackle this task with a keen and open heart.
delighted to discover all this new world has to offer.
despite the road's sinuous nature and its sporadic peaks,
I'll gear up to face any adversity and let my soul soar.

The soul's reveries

the remnants of my hometown encircle me still,
day after day, the same old faces float past.
its pull is strong, yet the walls won't let me fulfill
the urge to look beyond and wander away

torments of constant questioning: "when can I leave,
this place that confines my roaming, restless soul?"
the world beyond beckons, a siren's call to my heart,
promising adventures that will fulfill my essence.

a solo odyssey, evergreen memories to cherish,
experiences to carry for years, a precious trove.
serene landscapes, once merely dreams, now explored,
extending my reach and giving me a worldly scope

just a hint of enchantment, allows me to take wing,
to discover new faces, hear the stories they share.
weaving their tales into my own, I will bring
a patchwork of ties to placate my longing heart.

the allure of home still reigns, like a siren's melody
the pull of the unknown now fills me with greater fire.
I must heed this wanderlust, this deep, innate long -
to wander and discover the bliss my soul pines for.

True liberation

fanning the flames only opens the wound,
feeding a cycle where rage is consumed
the anger boils over, a bomb set to blow
time starts to tick, all ready to explode

obsessing over questions that linger unanswered,
craving the closure I feel I deserved
the chessboard's next move, the burrow's safe ground -
such temptations of conflict I try to leave behind.

the desire to treat them the same bitter way
a tit for tat, as the saying goes-
yet would it truly bring any joy in the end?
or leave me wallowing in "what could have been?"

releasing that craving for vengeance's sting,
as down that dark path lies only more suffering
although the hurt cuts deep, I refuse to return harm
rising above revenge with a heart sadly charmed

allowing myself liberation from damage once done
by choosing forgiveness, although hard earned
no longer swallowed by a cycle of strife
in order to embrace inner peace and reclaim my life

Renewal

the wounds that scarred you, they shan't define
your worth and spirit will transcend in time
those prior ailments, though sharp their sting
have a gifted perspective, an altered view to bring.
like petals emerging, obstinate but pure
breaking through the gloom, your resilience clear
no bitter wind can destroy your drive to bloom
for in the depths of your being, indelible strength awaits.
with each fragile unfolding, reveals deeper beauty
the breaking has ruptured, your soul self-healed.
move ahead from the agony that once carried you captive.
your true self is crowned at the flowering rebirth.

Unraveling stone

those walls once loomed tall and impenetrable
a fortress erected, my vulnerability to protect.
but in a moment of weakness, I let the barriers down,
thinking they could love the soul I had found.
what a fool I was, naïve and oblivious,
to believe my trust wouldn't be met with a cruel fate.
immaturity shone bright, an ugly lesson learnt,
as the river of my heart dried up, to stone it turned.
the walls grew taller, a vow to never let anyone near,
for I wouldn't be strong enough to step back from fear.
no longer would I worry about others disturbing my peace,
a happier life, where stress would cease to exist
time passed, and a warm, new face emerged
with the capacity to thaw the frost around my heart's blight.
but I stayed back, fear grasping me tightly.
haunted by memories of my dreadful past.
but a force drew us together, like magnets entangled.
and for a fleeting second, those walls began to unwind.
the foundations cracked, throwing balance into disorder.
a gleam of faith shone through the entrenched gray.
vulnerability beckoned, a risk I was afraid to take.
however, this soul's light jolted my heart awake.
to open up again, to feel the warmth inside,
or remain entombed, allowing the ice to win indefinitely?

Kindred souls

friends woven in transitory threads, transient at best.
their presence filled my life, yet desire remained unsatisfied.
longing for kindred hearts, a tie that won't fracture,
someone to be my platonic other half, come what may.

and suddenly, like a light in the darkest night:
I discovered my people, a gem of pure light.
a gift beyond measure, a treasure that cannot be bought.
laughter echoes across the world, bringing surprising delight.

a love so genuine, it needs no words to prove,
never questioning its depths, since it's a force that moves.
beyond the transactional, beyond the superficial airs,
a bond that outlasts comparisons, insecurities, and cares.

flaws and faults embraced, an ensemble to behold.
acceptance flows freely, leaving no heart unseen.
a warmth that envelops, a comfort that never fades.
a refuge from the crude winter, where real friendship thrives.

in their presence, I find solace and a home.
I am no longer a nomad, nor am I obliged to roam.
for in their embrace, I have met my lifelong friends.
a love that can survive the test of time and sin.

Missing pieces

a thousand miles from that treasured home.
a brand new universe unfolds before my eyes.
yet, even as fresh avenues inspire and goad,
my heart continues to yearn for familiar ways.

no guiding hands from mom and dad to hold,
the ones who helped me reach this lofty dream.
now left to conquer bizarre routes unknown,
to find my path across life's unknown waters.

this area they name my home, albeit far from it
its halls and rooms still lack that inviting ambience.
I desire the warmth of my family's comforting hug.
tender moments in our welcoming place.

the notion of home-cooked scents floating through
ignites a profound need in my soul.
why'd I forsake that familial tie?
as their warmth and love made me feel so whole.

but then loneliness descends again.
a garment of seclusion, thick in weight.
I count the days till I can travel back home.
return to the sanctuary of soothing rays.

those cherished breaks, for which my heart is aflame.
to bask again in kinship's lovely delight—
a reunion where I don't have to feel tame.
but we can bathe in the pure glow of familial affection.

Kinship revelations

irrespective of how swiftly the weeks depart by,
in my mind's eye, you will always be

a diminutive me, a beloved sight—
our family's lovely addition to see.

we wished upon stars in the night sky's embrace.
yet, how easily those sparkling years passed.

now standing before me, tall in your place,
I gaze at this grown visage of you.

when did you begin this transformation,
unfurl into one who can meet my gaze?

your own thoughts and opinions in formation,
sparking those fiery, sibling frays.

our perspectives no longer aligned,
but it's a sign you're becoming your own -

each visit uncovers more defined changes.
as into your selfhood, you're further grown.

the lengthening hair, the voice deepening still,
can't conceal the essence I've always known.

my heart reverberates with that primal thrill
of the child to whom I shall always be pulled.

though the natural seasons may constantly alter,
one core stays everlasting and unmoved:

the bond tying us as heaven's precious gift,
the you I've known and will always adore.

Savoring victories

rather than dwell on pursuits for *better*
I value each win that builds me afresh
relishing efforts where triumphs unfetter
grateful for the progress I have made it through

morning's first sips of thick coffee's balm
or a long, meandering walk through the park
each experience instills such quiet
as I truly embrace the present, I leave my mark

the melodies trilled by winged choristers
as they frolic amid blossom-cloaked trees
reminds us of nature's simplicity
to inspire via her intrinsic beauty

no grandeur scenes my soul's depths to move,
but the simple joys that each moment yields —
a petal's soft hue, a gentle breeze's crease,
unveiling the grace this Earth's charms reveal.

by sustaining life's humblest, loveliest moments,
I'm led to vistas of pure, permanent bliss.
in the small, I find fuel for my spirit's wings;
to rise beyond transitory filth and alloy.

each tiny triumph's warmth contributes to insulation.
the hearth of my being is flickering with delight.
living present and appreciative, fear finds no barrier.
just the brilliance of beauty at these times.

I hold to esteem every interaction I have
for who knows how ephemeral their presence will be?
a warm smile exchanged, kind words we nurture -
simple acts, yet tremendously meaningful we see.

these inspiring exchanges, bursts of pure light,
revive tired spirits, enabling them power to soar.
celebrating each small success makes daunting plight,
seems surmountable, with better days ahead.

with each humble triumph, an optimistic outlook
the terrain steadily changes throughout my voyage.
a potent feeling of achievement renews.
it provides propulsion as it ascends to higher elevations.

I share these moments of bliss, these crystallized lights.
letting their warm radiance amplify and permeate,
fulfilling this basic human need—our universal dreams.
to live a life full of illumination and magic.

reflecting on the events that set the road for progress,
provides perspective, a lens through which to discern.
the higher peaks my spirit longs to survey -
all souls truly crave for visions of love's truth.

Imbued in the now

always captivated by the immensity of the future,
a domain that I cannot control or conquer.
however, it lingers in the shadows of my consciousness

shadowing the here and now, transparency in the wake.
the only thing within my grasp, a tangible prize,
is the cyclical moment, scattered before my sight.

a trace of existence, fleeting yet real,
the one reality I can fully infuse with.
worries of what could have been, mere phantoms in the air,

dissipate like smoke, leaving not a care.
for at this moment, this breath, this fluttering heartbeat,
lies the power to embrace life, to truly unshutter.

the future is a moving illusion with no sway.
but the present, a canvas, where my soul is gifting
brushstrokes of vibrance, hues of lived experience,

creating a masterpiece, a life with true resonance.
freed from the constraints of what could occur,
I let the moments gather, standing firmly in the present.

as each moment is a treasure to admire and preserve.

Silver fox

I once feared the march of time
dreading the day my first silver strand appeared
an unwelcome line carved, a wrinkle's reminder.
that my youth's lovely freshness would soon fade.

the concept of the mirror's reflection, distorted
a face I could scarcely recall as my own.
memories of my prime like miraged oases,
longing to maintain that transitory self, forever shown.

but such prayers to stop nature's timeless cycles,
only feverish hopes against inescapable waves.
each fear of growing older, so irrational,
when nature's profound truth prevails in the cycle of change.

every dazzling thread is now pierced through with gray.
weave a tale about a life well lived.
tales to impart to those coming behind me,
of journeys traversed, lessons that are beautiful

the compulsion to camouflage, hide this transition
surrenders to the grace of aged elegance.
I welcome the new self that is ever-changing.
etch-lined recollections of hard-won permanency.

with each furrow engraved, each silver hair glistens,
comes a narrative ready to be unfurled —
of the heights I've scaled, depths I've plumbed and witnessed,
crafting a world of knowledge and charm.

Never gone too far

a parent's dire fear, a child's deepest dread,
to outlive those who nourished us, the roots from which we grew.
an atypical order, cosmic cruelty
watching wilted limbs fall from the family tree.

but a child's heart shatters, as parents fade away.
guardians, guides, and anchors, slipping with each passing day.
an irrational request, a plea to the divine.
to save us the sorrow of that heartbreaking line.

those who gave their all, unselfish and sincere
a sudden disappearance, leaving a fresh void.
corners, once warmed by their presence, now echo hollowly.
as memories become the only way we can take.

each revered second is a treasure trove to behold.
laughter, wisdom, and love, stories yet unspoken.
their legacy is imprinted in our souls,
a bittersweet comfort, as their pure essence entices.

though the physical form might wither and fade,
their spirits will eternally brighten our path.
continuing to flourish with their every breath,
for a parent's love, a child's bond surpass earthly life

Blessings in disguise

this heartfelt ode, expresses my gratitude,
to all who enriched my life with memorable days.
each encounter, whether favorable or painful,
has shaped the self that has now bloomed.

for had I not crossed those wandering roads,
emerged from valleys draped in sorrow's swathes,
the version of myself I have gotten to know
would be a mere specter, an unlived show.

despite the flaws that make me human
I have learned to offer them a warm caress.
accepting the entirety of who I am,
I embrace each gorgeous defect and grain.

the traumas once undergone, a crucible's fire,
reinforced my soul with mitigated dire--
allowing to face life's rough terrains
with steadfast courage, rising past the strains

my family's fierce love triumphed over all,
provide my life's greatest gifts; their aim.
though young, I failed to grasp the depths portrayed,
till the age-adorned sight never fades again.

now my purpose burns to offer the same grace,
providing as they did from that tender place.
to nurture by the unselfish love they provided,
life's most precious blessings continually remain

though valleys sank into sorrow's deepest caverns,
the dazzling delights we shared were eternal fires
outshone every fleeting ache this life has known.
illuminating the trajectory of my soul's evolution.

each experience, a brushstroke on the canvas,
gives me more vitality, more rejuvenation.
or this rich tapestry, gratitude is owed,
to all whose imprint has left me thus bestowed.

carrying a part of every soul who has touched my life,
woven into the fabric of my being.

Black Eagle Books

www.blackeaglebooks.org
info@blackeaglebooks.org

Black Eagle Books, an independent publisher, was founded as a nonprofit organization in April, 2019. It is our mission to connect and engage the Indian diaspora and the world at large with the best of works of world literature published on a collaborative platform, with special emphasis on foregrounding Contemporary Classics and New Writing.

www.ingramcontent.com/pod-product-compliance
Lightning Source LLC
Chambersburg PA
CBHW060621080526
44585CB00013B/936